**FASTBACK®** Crime and Detection

# The Blind Alley

## JOHN STEVENSON

**GLOBE FEARON**
Pearson Learning Group

# FASTBACK® CRIME AND DETECTION BOOKS

Beginner's Luck
**The Blind Alley**
Fun World
The Kid Who Sold Money
The Lottery Winner

No Loose Ends
Return Payment
The Setup
Small-Town Beat
Snowbound

**Cover** *t.r.* Eyewire/Getty Images, Inc.; *m.* Richard Hutchings/Richard Hutchings Photography. All photography © Pearson Education, Inc. (PEI) unless specifically noted.

Copyright © 2004 by Pearson Education, Inc., publishing as Globe Fearon®, an imprint of Pearson Learning Group, 299 Jefferson Road, Parsippany, NJ 07054. All rights reserved. No part of this book may be reproduced or transmitted in any form or by any means, electronic or mechanical, including photocopying, recording, or by any information storage and retrieval system, without permission in writing from the publisher. For information regarding permission(s), write to Rights and Permissions Department.

Globe Fearon® and Fastback® are registered trademarks of Globe Fearon, Inc.

ISBN 0-13-024491-0
Printed in the United States of America
1 2 3 4 5 6 7 8 9 10     07 06 05 04 03

1-800-321-3106
www.pearsonlearning.com

I sat in my chair and studied the gold lettering on the window. It read: JAMES KATT, INVESTIGATIONS. The three deep scratches in the lettering had been made by my partner, Gregory. He'd been chasing a fly—and missed.

Gregory is a black cat. He moved into the office a day or so after I did. And he decided to stay, though I still don't know why. Maybe he likes dusty rooms filled with old furniture.

Footsteps in the hall got my mind off the lettering. The person was moving slowly. Then the doorknob turned.

"Come in," I called. As the door opened, Gregory leaped from the top of the filing cabinet to the windowsill.

A large black dog entered. It was leading a man wearing dark glasses.

I jumped up and hurried around my desk. "Let me help you," I said, pushing a pile of magazines off the visitor's chair. I took his elbow while the dog sniffed at my ankles.

My blind visitor put his hand out and said, "I'm Willard Barclay."

I shook his hand. Then I moved back behind my desk. The office was a mess, but I didn't imagine Mr. Barclay was going to notice that. "What can I do for you?" I asked.

"I want to hire you," the blind man answered.

"That's nice to know," I said. "I work for $200 a day plus expenses. Before I start, I need one day's pay in advance. And I will not do anything that's against the law. So, what is it you want me to do?"

"I want you to make a payoff for me."

A payoff. It sounded as if Barclay had some big trouble on his hands. "A payoff for blackmail?" I asked.

"Right," he said, pushing his dark glasses back on his short nose. "You could say that my sins are catching up with me."

"That's the usual reason," I said. "But let me warn you about blackmail payoffs.

There's often no end to them. Blackmailers have a bad habit of coming back for more and more. Maybe the best thing for you to do is talk to the police."

"Would I be here if I wanted to talk to the police?" he asked. "The police ask a lot of questions. And their work has a way of getting into the newspapers. I certainly don't need my private life dragged out for a public showing. I don't need my friends crossing the street when they see me coming. I'm here for *your* help."

Things had been real slow lately, and I needed Barclay's business. So I let the whole subject of the police drop. "May I ask you something, Mr. Barclay?" I said. "How did you happen to pick me for this job? And how did you find my office?"

I couldn't think of anyone who might have sent him to me. Even my best friend, Dave Willows of the Los Angeles Police Department, has the bad manners to laugh at my business.

"Well, I didn't stick a pin in a page of the telephone book," Willard Barclay answered. "But I did the next best thing. I called a cab and had the driver look in the phone book. He read me all the names listed under private investigators. When he got to your name, I just decided on you. I've always been an animal lover. I had a dog long before Blackie. And I figured that with a name like yours, you, too, must be an animal lover. The cabdriver brought me over here and let me off at the foot of your stairs."

I paused for a moment and thought about what he had said. I couldn't quite follow his reasoning, but I was glad he liked the name Katt.

"Just what is it you want me to do?" I asked.

"I want you to pick me up this evening and drive me over to the meeting place," he said. "After that, I want you to pretend you're me and hand over the briefcase with the money. You'll be given an envelope in return for the briefcase."

"What exactly are you buying, Mr. Barclay?" I asked. "What is the blackmailer giving you in return for the payoff?"

Barclay put a scowl on his face. "Pictures," he said through tight lips. "This man says he has some pictures of me taken a long time ago. Before I lost my sight."

"And you think he does?"

"There's a good possibility. There was a time in my life when I did some things I'm not very proud of. I can't take the chance. I've got to pay him."

"Are you paying for the negatives, too?"

"Of course," he snapped. "I'd be a darn fool not to demand them as well."

"He could easily have made another set of pictures," I pointed out.

"I know that," he replied. "But I have to believe him when he says he's just interested in one payoff."

"Where do I fit in?" I wanted to know.

"I want you to check the envelope before

the man gets the briefcase. Just act as if you're counting the pictures and negatives. He'll be expecting me to do that. But while you count, check them out. Make sure they're what I'm paying for. If they aren't, I want you to stop the exchange. Walk away with the briefcase."

"How will I know if I have the right pictures?"

"They'll show me sitting in a restaurant with two or three men. I'm sure you'll recognize them. They're well-known criminals. I had to borrow money from them a long time ago. To rescue my business. If word gets out that I even knew them at all, I'll be ruined. The government will come down hard on me."

"And if the pictures are not in the envelope?"

"Put some pressure on the blackmailer. Tell him that we don't have a deal unless he promises to *deliver* the pictures the next time. The fact that you're there to protect my interests should show him something. Just because I'm blind, it doesn't mean I'm a fool."

I sat back in my chair and thought about it. It seemed to be a pretty good plan. Barclay wasn't stupid. But he was desperate. He wanted to get out of this mess so badly that he was willing to trust even a blackmailer. Up to a point. It sounded as if it could be dangerous for me. I didn't mind. There's always a little danger in every job I take.

I had one more question for Barclay. "What makes you think I can pass for you?" I asked him.

"Do you look anything like me at all?" he asked.

"Well, we appear to be about the same height and the same age. You're probably 20 pounds heavier than I am."

"That should certainly be good enough," he said. "You'll be wearing my dark glasses and Blackie will be leading you. The blackmailer isn't going to be studying you. The briefcase is what he's after."

"Will Blackie lead me?" I asked.

"He'll do what I tell him to do," Barclay replied. "Now are you going to take the job or not? I can't waste the day here."

"Sure," I said before he could tell Blackie it was time to leave. "What time do I pick you up and where?"

"I don't want you to come to my house," he said quickly. "My wife has a friend who comes over to play cards with her. The friend will be there at eight. So I will leave at 7:45 for a walk with Blackie. I will meet you at the corner two blocks south of my house."

He pulled a wallet from his pants pocket and reached inside it. "This has my address on it," he said, passing me a card. "Now I'll give you your fee."

He took a pack of twenties from his wallet and started to count them out. When he got to ten, he said, "That's two hundred, and here's another twenty for gas."

I thought about telling him that the price of gas had gone down, but decided against it. "Thanks," I said, "but that's not right. The third bill you counted out was a fifty."

I found the fifty and pushed it into his hand.

"You're quite right," he said, showing enough teeth to make me think he was smiling. "I just wanted to make sure you were honest."

I smiled back, wondering if he knew about the gas. He put the fifty back into his wallet and waved another twenty at me. I grabbed it. "You will be carrying $5,000 of my money," he said. "So you must excuse me for checking up on you."

"That's all right," I told him. "It doesn't hurt to be safe. Now, can I get you a cab?"

"The driver who brought me is waiting downstairs," he said. "But thank you just the same. I'll meet you at 7:50 tonight."

I watched as Blackie led him toward the door. I stood by my office window and saw them get into the waiting cab. They looked as if they'd never have any trouble going anywhere. Just then, Gregory leaped onto my shoulder. Maybe he was hungry. Or maybe he was glad to see Blackie off. There's no telling what's in Gregory's head.

At six o'clock that evening, I headed for my apartment. I wanted to change my clothes. Besides, I was getting tired of talking to Gregory. What did he know about blackmailers?

At home, I thought about eating, but decided against it. Gregory and I had munched on some potato chips during the afternoon. I changed into an old suit that seemed better for trips down dark alleys. Then I hid away most of the money Barclay had given me. I couldn't afford to be robbed by the blackmailer.

Before I left, I loaded my .38 automatic and strapped on my holster. I didn't plan on shooting anybody. But in my line of work, you never know when you'll need a little extra protection.

By 7:40, I was sitting in my car waiting for Barclay. The neighborhood two blocks south of his house was a good one. I guessed that he lived in a nice home. I wondered exactly what business Barclay was in. Whatever it was, it was a better living than being a private investigator.

My mind stopped wandering when I heard Barclay. In truth, I didn't hear him, because he was wearing rubber-soled shoes. I heard Blackie's claws tapping on the car door. "Is that you, Katt?" Barclay said.

"I'll be right there," I replied, jumping out of the car and heading for the passenger side.

Getting Barclay into the car was easy. He settled into the seat with the briefcase on his lap. He had a walking cane with him. Somehow, Blackie curled up at his feet. I figured they'd both be more comfortable in the back seat, but Barclay wanted to sit up front. And he was paying.

The address he gave me was in Venice. We were in West Los Angeles, so it was only about a 10-minute ride to the street he wanted. "The ocean is off to your right, isn't it?" he asked when we arrived.

"Just as you said," I replied.

"Now get out of the car and come around to my side. I'll give you the briefcase and let Blackie out. Carry the briefcase in your right hand."

I got out of the car and moved around to the passenger side. I opened the car door and took the briefcase from him. "Take Blackie's harness in your left hand," he said, handing it to me as the dog stepped onto the street. "When you get past the second house, there will be an alley. Go down the alley, and a man will be waiting to take the briefcase and give you the envelope. When it's all over, come back here and drive me home again." Barclay patted the dog and said, "Blackie, walk, just walk, boy."

Blackie had good ears. I had to hold him back until I had Barclay's dark glasses. I slipped them on and loosened my hold on

Blackie. He took off and went for the alley as if it were home. I was glad he was along, because seeing with the dark glasses wasn't all that easy. I gathered Barclay didn't clean them very often.

Blackie led me halfway down that alley and stopped. He wouldn't move. "You're just supposed to walk, boy," I told him. "What's the matter?"

If he answered, I didn't hear him. I didn't hear anything. Something like a house landed on my head. I felt myself falling. And before I passed out, I felt someone pulling the briefcase from my hand.

I don't know how long I was out. But when I came back to life, the lump on my head felt as if it had been growing there for years. I took a few deep breaths and pulled the dark glasses from my eyes. Not only was the briefcase gone, the dog was, too. I hoped he'd gone back to Barclay.

After a couple of bad starts, I got to my feet and looked around. There was a shorter alley off to my right leading to a side street. The smells from a Chinese restaurant right behind me reminded me I hadn't eaten dinner. I shook my head. It really hurt. I owed somebody a thank-you. And Barclay was going to tell me who that somebody was.

When I reached my car, I saw that Barclay wasn't going to tell me a thing. He was gone.

Something about all this was starting to bother me. I pulled out the card with Barclay's address on it. I figured I'd check to see if he'd made it home. But for the moment, he could wait. I needed to know one other thing before I looked for him.

By the time I reached Barclay's house, an ambulance was pulling away. I parked across the street and spotted Dave Willows's police car in front of Barclay's house.

There was a uniformed cop at the door. He knew Dave and I were friends, so he let me pass inside. Barclay was sitting on a couch with Blackie resting in front of him. Dave Willows was standing nearby. "What's going on here?" I asked.

Dave smiled. "Just the man I was going

to send for," he answered. "Mr. Barclay tells me you've been working for him."

"That's right," I said, "but what's the trouble?"

"Mrs. Barclay was murdered earlier this evening," Dave said. "A friend of hers who stopped by to play cards found her. From the looks of the place, I gather the Barclays were robbed, too."

"That's terrible," I said to Barclay, wondering if he'd told Willows about the blackmailer.

"Yes, it is," Barclay replied.

I couldn't help noticing that he had on another pair of dark glasses. "Are you all right?" I asked him.

"As all right as I can be considering what's happened," he answered. "You and I can discuss our business at a later time, OK?"

From his words, I knew he hadn't told Willows about the blackmailer. Willows heard the same words. "Discuss what?" he asked.

"Sergeant Willows," Barclay said, "as I told you before, that's a matter between me and Mr. Katt. It has nothing to do with my wife's murder. And questioning both of us isn't going to help you find the murderer."

Willows looked at me and shook his head. "I'll decide that, Mr. Barclay," he said, before turning to me. "Jim, were you with Barclay before eight?"

"Yes," I said, "I met him around 7:50. When was Mrs. Barclay murdered?"

"Somewhere around then," he answered. "But we might not be able to fix the time exactly. Anyway, that's not important. Mr. Barclay isn't a suspect. Unless, of course, whatever you were working on for him had something to do with Mrs. Barclay. Did it?"

"Not really," Barclay said, answering for me.

Willows looked my way. "I don't think so," I replied.

"Maybe we should go down to the station and talk about it," Willows said.

I didn't like that suggestion coming from the mouth of my friend. But I realized he was just doing his job. "If Mr. Barclay was telling me the truth, it had nothing to do with his wife," I said.

"OK," Willows said. "I guess I'll be going, unless there's something I can do for you, Mr. Barclay."

The lump on my head was beginning to hurt again. And I was just about sure who had put it there.

"Wait a minute," I said before Barclay could answer Dave. "I think talking to Mr. Barclay might do the both of us some good."

"What's that supposed to mean?" Barclay asked.

"Just that I'd like to know what happened to you tonight out in Venice. Where did you go? And don't you care what happened to *me*—and your briefcase and its contents?"

"Well, yes, . . . but after what's happened to my wife, how can I be expected to think of that now?"

"Mr. Barclay," I said, "it didn't even concern you *before* you found out what happened to your wife. You just took off. In case you're interested, someone knocked me out in the alley. When I woke up, the briefcase was gone—and so was Blackie."

"Blackie came back to me at the car," Barclay said. "When you didn't return with him, I had him lead me into the alley. I called your name several times, but you didn't answer. I figured the blackmailer took off with the briefcase but didn't deliver the goods. And so you went after him."

Willows spoke up—angrily. "Since you two are discussing this *now*, will someone fill me in on what's going on?" There's no one more upset than a cop who's being left in the dark. And Dave was pure cop.

"Mr. Barclay hired me to make a blackmail payoff for him tonight," I said. "I was supposed to pretend I was him. Before I could get the goods from the blackmailer, someone knocked me out."

"What do you mean 'someone'?" Barclay asked. "Surely it was the blackmailer."

"I don't think so," I said.
"Who then?"
"You, Mr. Barclay," I replied.

"*Me?*" Barclay said in shock. "Why would I knock you out? And how?"

"You knocked me out to make your story more convincing. A blackmailer stealing your money without giving you what you were paying for in return. You thought I'd wake up and start looking for some mysterious man who conked me on the head. But there never was a blackmailer. You made the whole story up."

"You're crazy!" Barclay said.

"Why would he do that?" Dave wanted to know.

"Because *he* killed his wife here before he ever met me tonight. He was just trying to use our appointment as an alibi. But he knew no one would be showing up to take the briefcase from me. So, he had to knock me out and take it himself. It made the whole story more believable."

"It's all a lie," Barclay said.

"Take it easy, Mr. Barclay," Dave said. Then to me he said, "Can you prove any of this, Jim?"

"Well, I can prove a couple of things," I said. "One, Barclay never intended for *me* to drive him back here tonight as he told me. You see, he made one or two mistakes. He asked the cabdriver who drove him to my office today to meet him in Venice tonight. He gave the driver a street corner address just one block from the alley where

I left him. So Barclay knew this *afternoon* that he would need a ride tonight. Because he was planning on leaving me out cold in the alley."

"How do you know all this?" Dave asked.

"I checked it out," I said. "When I got back to the car and saw that Barclay was gone, I got suspicious. Why would he leave without me—and how? So, on a hunch, I stopped at the cab company before I came here. Since I saw him leaving my office today, I knew which company to check. The driver remembered Mr. Barclay all right. After all, he's blind and he gives *very* good tips."

"That still doesn't prove anything," Barclay said. "You claim I knocked you out. How could I have done that? *You* had my dog."

"Yeah, that bothered me for a while," I admitted. "But when Blackie and I were walking down the alley, he suddenly stopped at one spot without a word from me. I thought that was strange. It was as if he'd been rehearsed into doing that—as if he'd been walked down that alley before and knew just where to stop. And he had been—with you.

"You probably walked him to that spot several times," I went on. "You knew we'd be standing right there. It wasn't hard for you to find. The alley crosses another shorter one at that point. After I left you at the car, you just walked around the block and cut through the short alley. You used your cane as a guide. The restaurant kitchen at that spot made it even easier to find, given your sense of smell."

"What about the briefcase?" Dave asked.

I looked at Barclay. He was beginning to sweat a little. "That was the final mistake he made," I said. "I found it. I have it out in my car."

"*What?*" Barclay said.

"He had the cabdriver drop him off two blocks from here," I said. "I stopped off at the same spot. I found the briefcase in a garbage can in another alley right where he got out. It was in plain sight. He probably never figured anyone would be looking there for it."

"What about the money?" Dave asked.

"Well, the case is locked. But I'll bet if we open it, there won't be any $5,000 in it. What do you say, Mr. Barclay? Did you throw out your briefcase with all that money inside?"

"That's enough," Barclay said, finally cracking. "I killed her. I had to. You don't know how she treated me. But no one will convict a blind man for murder. You'll see."

"Yes, we'll see," Dave Willows said. "But before you say anything else, Mr. Barclay, let me read you your rights."

I tried to listen to Dave reading Barclay his rights. But my head was hurting bad. I needed to leave. Besides, I didn't want Barclay asking for his money back.

JOHN STEVENSON *has written more than 20 crime and suspense novels and is an international award-winning short story author.*